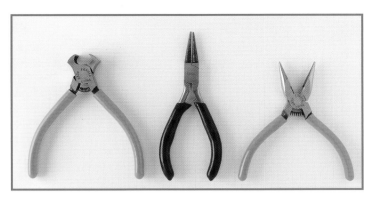

Basic Tools

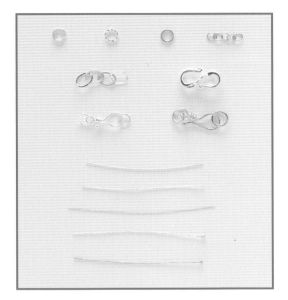

Basic Findings

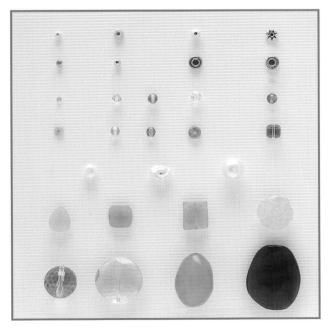

Basic Beads

It's hard to believe that this sparkling necklace was made with a pair of pliers, a bit of silver chain, a clasp and beads strung on head pins. This is a very good project for the first-time jewelry maker.

Part of the fun of making your own necklace is that no one will have one just like yours. You can change the bead sizes, colors, and shapes to vary the look without having to work out a new design. You can also make the silver chain shorter to create a matching bracelet.

If you love these projects, check out Mary's wonderful companion books, Beautiful Bracelets and Eclectic Earrings.

Novelty Necklaces

Make One for Every Day of the Week!

Citrus Necklace
see pages 6 - 7

Crystal Cluster
see pages 12 - 13

Twilight
see pages 14 - 15

Ocean Sunrise
see pages 8 - 9

Crystal & Pearl
see pages 10 - 11

Ruby Red
see pages 16 - 17

Blue Suede
see pages 18 - 19

Pick up a split ring and carefully thread the hook part of the clasp on it as shown above.

Be careful not to pry the split ring too far apart as it may stretch and not spring back into position.

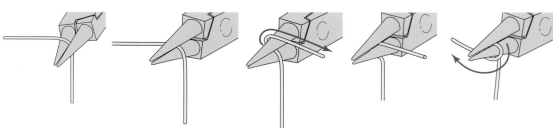

Cut a 4" long piece of 22 gauge wire. Grasp the wire with round-nose pliers about 1¼" from the top. Bend the wire at a 90° angle. Loosen your grip on the pliers and pivot them from horizontal to vertical. • Wrap the short piece of wire over the top jaw of the pliers. • Reposition the wire on the bottom jaw of the pliers. Complete the loop by wrapping the short end of the wire around the bottom jaw of the pliers.

Citrus Necklace

Link loops together to make a necklace of delicious citrus colors!

MATERIALS:
72" of 22 gauge Sterling wire (D)
10 flat 10mm square Olive jade beads (G)
4 flat 10mm x 12mm Orange chalcedony beads (H)
15 round 4mm Amber beads (F)
22 Olive jade 4mm disks (E)
2 Yellow jade 15mm carved flower beads (I)
16mm x 24mm new jade nugget bead (J)
3 Silver 5mm split rings (B)
Silver hook and eye clasp (A)
1½" Sterling ball headpin (C)
round-nose pliers

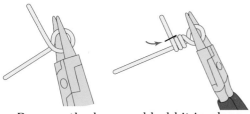

Remove the loop and hold it in place.

Without touching the long end of the wire, begin coiling the shorter piece of wire around the longer piece. Begin the coils as close to the loop as possible. Make two or three coils, then clip the end of wire close to the coils.

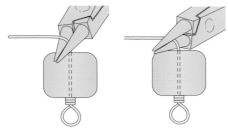

Thread on a square Olive jade bead. Grasp the wire with the pliers about ⅛" from the end of the jaws. Bend the wire at a 90° angle as shown below.

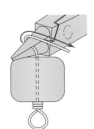

Pivot pliers from horizontal to vertical. Wrap the wire around the top jaw of the pliers as shown below.

Move the piece to the bottom jaw of the pliers and complete the loop as shown.

Before coiling, thread the split ring attached to the hook along the wire until it snaps into the loop. Grasp the loop with the pliers and coil the wire around the neck two or three times. Clip the wire close to the coils.

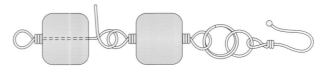

Cut another 4" piece of wire and make a wrapped loop on one end. Thread on another square Olive jade bead and make a loop in the other end. Instead of threading the split ring through the open loop, thread on the bottom loop of the previous link.

Follow diagram at the left to complete this half of the necklace.

Repeat for the second half of the necklace beginning with the closed ring instead of the hook.

 Thread the beads for the pendant on the head pin as shown at left. Make a wrapped loop at the top of the head pin.

Connect the two necklace halves and the pendant with a split ring.

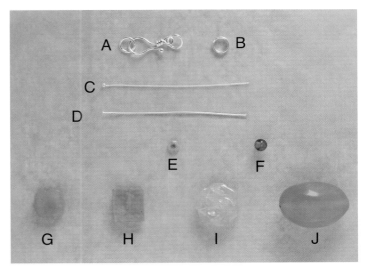

A simple strand of pink pearls and mother of pearl dangles lets you wear the lovely colors of sunrise around your neck!

MATERIALS:
16" strand of Dark Pink 4mm x 5mm oval pearls (A)
13 Pink 12mm mother of pearl disks (B)
27 bali 3mm Silver daisy spacers (D)
13 Sterling 1½" head pins (G)
1 Sterling hook and eye clasp (F)
2 crimp tubes (C)
2 Sterling 6mm split rings (E)
24" of beading wire (H)
round-nose pliers
chain-nose pliers

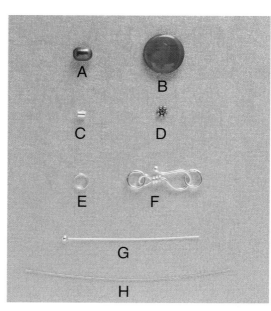

Ocean Sunrise

Thread a mother of pearl disk and a Silver daisy spacer bead on a head pin. Grasp the pin as close to the spacer bead as possible. Bend the wire at a 90° angle.

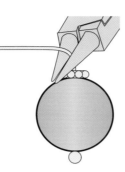

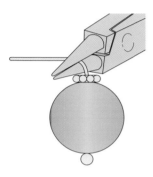

Loosen your grip on the pliers and pivot them from horizontal to vertical. Apply pressure to the pliers again when your work looks like this illustration.

Wrap the end of the pin over the top jaw of the pliers as shown.

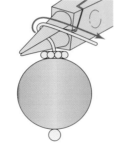

Reposition the wire on the bottom jaw of the pliers. Complete the loop by wrapping the short end of the wire around the bottom jaw of the pliers.

Remove the loop and hold it in place as shown at right. Without touching the beads on the pin, begin coiling the wire around the pin. Begin the coils as close to the loop as possible. Make two or three coils, then clip the end of wire close to the coils as shown at right. Make 12 more dangles.

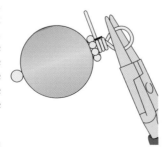

Thread the disks, pearls and Silver spacers on the beading wire referring to photo.

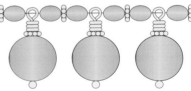

Divide the remaining pearls into two groups - string one group on either side of the center section.

Thread the closed ring attached to the hook of your clasp onto a split ring. Be careful not to pry the split ring too far apart as it may stretch and not spring back into position.

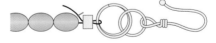

Thread a crimp tube on the wire. Thread the wire through the split ring and then back through the crimp tube. Flatten the crimp by squeezing it with pliers.

Repeat the process for the closed ring on the other side of necklace.

Clip the wire close to the flattened crimp on each side.

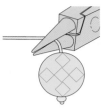 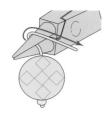 

Loosen your grip on the pliers and pivot them from horizontal to vertical. Apply pressure to the pliers again when your work looks like the left illustration above.

Wrap the wire over the top jaw of the pliers.

Reposition the wire on the bottom jaw of the pliers.

  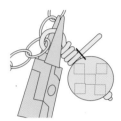

Wrap the wire around the bottom jaw of the pliers.

Slip the loop on the center link of the chain.

Hold the loop in place and begin coiling the wire around the neck. Begin coils as close to the loop as possible. Make 2-3 coils, then clip the end of wire close to the coils.

Make 2 more large dangles using stardust rondels and 20 mm disks. Attach them to the fifth link from the center on each side of the chain.

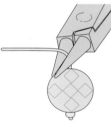

To make large center dangle, place a 4mm star-dust bead, a 2mm disk and a 20mm Aqua faceted glass disk bead on a ball head pin. Grasp head pin with round-nose pliers about ⅛" above the bead. Bend at a 90˚ angle.

Make 2 dangles each using 4mm stardust, 9mm faceted and a 4mm stardust rondell. Attach to third link from center on each side of chain.

Make 2 dangles each using 3mm stardust and a 9mm faceted bead.

Attach to the seventh link from center on each side of chain. Make a dangle with each briolet and 3" of wire.

Attach dangles to the links centered between the faceted bead dangles and wrap the loop.

Make a dangle with each of the pearls. Attach a pearl dangle to the link on each side of the briolets.

On one side of necklace, attach 3 dangles in each of the 2 links after the last faceted bead dangle and one and the next link.

Repeat for other side of necklace.

Attach the S hook to ends of necklace.

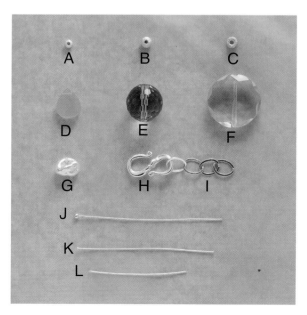

MATERIALS:
28 irregular center-drilled disk pearls (G)
Six 9mm x 11mm Blue chalcedony flat briolets (D)
Three 20mm Aqua faceted glass disk beads (F)
Four 9mm Aqua faceted glass round beads (E)
Three 4mm and two 3mm stardust beads (A, B)
Two 4mm rondell stardust beads (C)
19" of Sterling Silver chain with 8mm x 6mm links (I)
13mm Sterling Silver S hook (H)
28 flat 26 gauge head pins (K)
7 ball 26 gauge head pins (J)
15" of 26 gauge Sterling Silver wire (L)
wire cutters
round nose pliers
chain nose pliers

Crystal & Pearl

Use faceted beads the color of a glacial lake, lustrous pearls and shimmering silver chain to create a one-of-a-kind masterpiece!

Crystal Cluster

Clusters of crystals
nestle between stone
nugget beads to make
a glimmering
fashion statement!

MATERIALS:
20 stone nuggets - we used 12mm x 20mm dyed jade (J)
20 4mm crystal bicones & rounds in peridot and rose (A-D)
20 6mm crystal bicones & rounds in peridot and rose (E-H)
2 10mm x 10mm hill tribe silver beads (I)
40 2" sterling silver head pins (L)
45mm Hill tribe silver flower pendant
20" of beading wire (K)
sterling silver toggle (M)
two silver crimp tubes
wire cutters
round-nose pliers
chain-nose pliers

The necklace shown is 18" long.

Thread a crystal on a head pin. Grasp the pin with pliers about ⅛" from the end of the jaws. The pliers should be touching the top of the crystal. Bend the wire at a 90° angle.

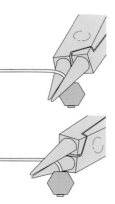

Pivot the pliers from horizontal to vertical.

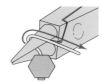

Wrap the wire around the top jaw of your pliers.

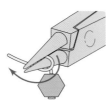

Reposition the wire on the bottom jaw of the pliers. Wrap the wire around the bottom jaw of the pliers.

Grasp the loop of the dangle with the pliers. Without touching the crystal, begin coiling the short end around the neck of the dangle. Begin coils as close to the loop as possible. Make two or three coils, then clip the end of the wire close to the coils.

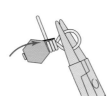

Repeat steps 1 through 5 for a total of 40 crystal dangles.

To make a cluster:

Thread on a nugget. Thread on five 4mm and five 6mm dangles. Thread on another nugget. When the nuggets are pushed together, the dangles gather up to form a cluster between them.

Follow illustration below for beading pattern of necklace.
Adjust the number of beads to make your necklace the desired length.

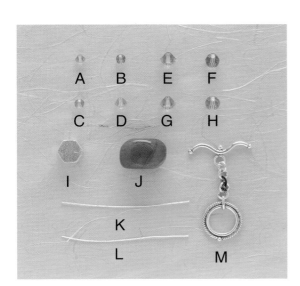

Attaching the clasp:

Thread one end of the wire through a crimp tube. Pass the wire through one end of the toggle clasp and then back through the crimp tube and a few beads of the necklace. Flatten the crimp with chain-nose pliers as shown below.

Trim the excess wire.

Repeat for the other end of the necklace.

Pick up a split ring and carefully thread the hook part of the clasp on it as shown above. Be careful not to pry the split ring too far apart as it may stretch and not spring back into position.

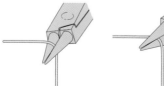 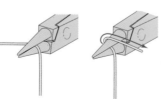 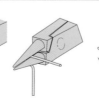

Cut a 4" long piece of 22 gauge wire. Grasp the wire with round-nose pliers about $1^1/4$" from the top. Bend the wire at a 90° angle. • Loosen your grip on the pliers and pivot them from horizontal to vertical. • Wrap the short piece of wire over the top jaw of the pliers. • Reposition the wire on the bottom jaw of the pliers. • Complete the loop by wrapping the short end of the wire around the bottom jaw of the pliers. • Remove the loop and hold it in place as shown at right. • Without touching the long end of the wire, begin coiling the shorter piece of wire around the longer piece. Begin the coils as close to the loop as possible. Make two or three coils, then clip the end of wire close to the coils.

Twilight

The soothing colors of a late evening sky grace this elegant tasseled necklace!

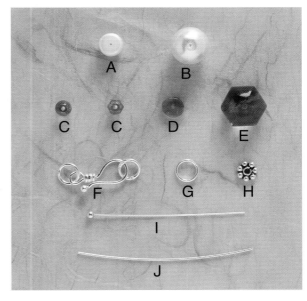

MATERIALS:
76" of 24 gauge Sterling wire (J)
28 Green 4mm fire polish beads (C)
8 Amethyst 5mm disks (D)
42 Silver 5mm daisy spacers (H)
7 Swarovski 10mm pearls (B)
2 5mm cultured pearls (A)
6 Fluorite 10mm melon beads (E)
3 Sterling 6mm split rings (G)
1 Sterling hook and eye clasp (F)
3 Sterling 2" ball head pins (I)
round-nose pliers

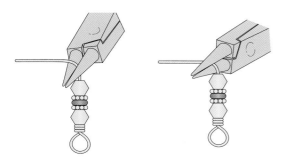

Thread on a small round Green bead, Silver spacer, an Amethyst disk, Silver spacer and another Green bead. Grasp the wire with pliers about ⅛" from the end of the jaws. Bend the wire at a 90° angle.

Pivot the pliers from horizontal to vertical just as before.

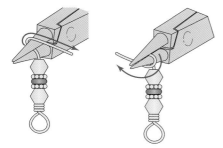

Wrap the wire around the top jaw of the pliers.

Move the piece to the bottom jaw of the pliers and complete the loop.

Before you begin coiling, thread the split ring attached to the hook along the wire until it snaps into the loop.

Grasp the loop with the pliers and coil the wire around the neck two or three times. Clip the wire close to the coils.

Cut another 4" piece of wire and repeat steps 2 through 12. Instead of threading the split ring through the open loop, thread on the bottom loop of the previous link as shown at right.

Follow the diagram at left to complete the first half of the necklace.

Repeat for the second half of the necklace - attach the closed ring to the split ring to begin.

To make the dangles that hang from the bottom of the pendant thread the beads shown at left on each of three head pins. Make a wrapped loop with a long neck at the top of the pin. (The longer neck is made by grasping the head pin near the base of the jaws instead of near the tip.) Make approximately 6 coils with the end of the pin.

To make the pendant, cut a 4" piece of wire and make a wrapped loop with a short neck. Thread on the beads for the pendant as shown.

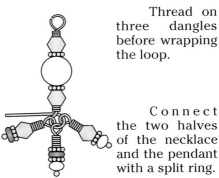

Thread on three dangles before wrapping the loop.

Connect the two halves of the necklace and the pendant with a split ring.

Ruby Red

Lovely ruby red faceted glass beads in irregular shapes are capped with gold beads and connected with gold loops and rings!

MATERIALS:
7 assorted red, flat irregular shaped faceted glass beads (A)
16 gold 6mm disk beads (D)
16 gold 3mm round beads (B)
24" of gold 22 gauge wire (G)
12" of round-link gold chain (E)
3" gold head pin (H)
small gold hook and ring clasp (F)
2 gold 5mm split rings (C)
wire cutters
round-nose pliers
chain-nose pliers

Grasp a 4" length of 22 gauge wire with round-nose pliers about 1¼" from the end. Bend at a 90° angle.

Loosen your grip on the pliers and pivot them from horizontal to vertical. Apply pressure to the pliers again when it looks like illustration at right.

Wrap the wire over the top jaw of the pliers.

Reposition the wire on the bottom jaw of the pliers. Wrap the wire around the bottom jaw of the pliers.

Slip the loop on the last link of a 1" piece of chain.

Hold the loop in place and begin coiling the wire around the neck. Begin the coils as close to the loop as possible.

Make two or three coils, then clip the end of wire close to the coils.

Thread a 3mm round, a 6mm gold disk, a faceted red glass bead, a 6mm gold disk and another 3mm round bead on the remaining wire. Make a wrapped loop just as you did for the opposite end referring to the illustrations below..

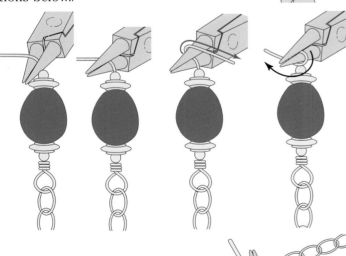

Slip the end link in another 1" piece of chain into the loop before coiling the short end of the wire around the neck.

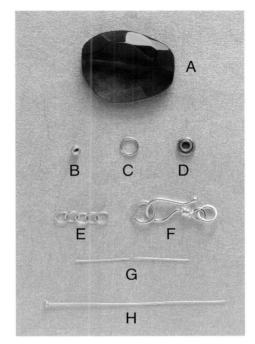

Add two more groups of gold and faceted glass beads connected by 1" pieces of chain. Then add a 3mm round, 6mm disk and 3mm round connected to the last link of a 2" piece of chain. Attach the clasp to the last link of the chain with a split ring.

Repeat steps 1 through 12 to complete the second half of the necklace.

Make the pendant:
Thread a 3mm round, a 6mm gold disk, a faceted red glass bead, a 6mm gold disk and another 3mm round bead on the 3" head pin. Make a wrapped loop at the top.

Join the two halves of the necklace and the pendant with a split ring.

Blue Suede Necklace

MATERIALS:
7 Swarovski 10 mm pearls (F)
3 Swarovski 6 mm cubes (E)
2 Swarovski 5 mm nail heads (C)
3 Swarovski 4 mm bicones (A)
2 Swarovski 4mm rounds (B)
24" of 22 gauge Sterling wire (I)
40" of Blue suede (H)
5 twisted 6mm jump rings (D)
11 Sterling 1$^{1}/_{2}$" ball head pins (G)
round nose pliers

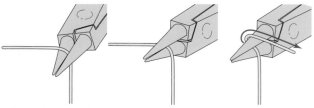

To make pearl links:
Cut a 4" long piece of 22 gauge wire. Grasp the wire with round-nose pliers about 1$^{1}/_{4}$" from the top. Bend the wire at a 90° angle. • Loosen your grip on the pliers and pivot them from horizontal to vertical. • Wrap the short piece of wire over the top jaw of the pliers as shown. • Reposition the wire on the bottom jaw of the pliers. • Complete the loop by wrapping the short end of the wire around the bottom jaw of the pliers. • Remove the loop and hold it in place as shown.